Friends & Inclusion

Five Approaches to
Building Relationships

Peggy Hutchison & John Lord
with Karen Lord

INCLUSION

Library and Archives Canada Cataloguing in Publication

Hutchison, Peggy, 1950-
    Friends & inclusion : five approaches to building relationships
/ Peggy Hutchison & John Lord with Karen Lord.

Includes bibliographical references.
ISBN 978-1-895418-95-8

    1. Friendship. 2. Social integration. 3. Interpersonal relations.
4. People with disabilities--Social networks. 5. People with
disabilities--Family relationships. 6. Parents of children with
disabilities. I. Lord, John, 1943- II. Lord, Karen, 1978- III. Title.
IV. Title: Friends and inclusion.

BJ1533.F8H88 2010   302.3'4087   C2010-904716-8

An Inclusion Press Book
Published by Inclusion Press   Copyright © 2010 Inclusion Press

Printed in Canada by Couto Printing and Publishing Services
Printed on stock containing post consumer recycled content

Cover Photo: Photographer: John Lord
Back Cover Photo: Photographer: Tim Hutchison

INCLUSION PRESS
47 Indian Trail, Toronto,
Ontario Canada M6R 1Z8
p. 416.658.5363 f. 416.658.5067
e. inclusionpress@inclusion.com

inclusion.com   BOOKS • WORKSHOPS • MEDIA • RESOURCES

Contents

Preface

The importance of relationships cannot be overstated. However, our busy and often complex lives leave little time or energy for developing relationships that are integral to a nurturing society. Many people, such as those with disabilities, often have to be so concerned about meeting their basic needs that they can devote little time to relationships. Arguably, many people in Canadian and other western societies are at risk of slipping through the cracks, and experiencing social isolation and alienation. The reason for writing this book is to address this issue and to propose some solutions to this problem.

People who are at risk are often seen by the public, community organizations, and families as first and foremost needing services and the help of professionals. While this response is sometimes useful, it can impede the development of meaningful friendships. Our society for the most part still assumes that people with disabilities mostly require services rather than a rich life in community with friends.

The opportunity to have real friends occurs through participation in family, school, neighbourhoods, and other places where people gather. Real friendships are genuine caring relationships where people share common interests, love and respect each other, and want to spend time together. Contrary to the idea that these kinds of friendships can only happen naturally, our experience is that discovering and building real friendships often requires intentional or deliberate action.

For some people, a textured life rich with friends is like a beautifully woven cloth. The impression initially might be that there is certain simplicity but closer examination reveals a complexity. The color, design, and the grain are all orchestrated in a way that brings wonder. This fabric has been created intentionally because of a dream, creativity, and persistence.

This book reflects on the question of friendship first in the context of broader society and second specifically with regard to our daughter, Karen Lord. This book is written from a parent and family perspective by Karen's parents, Peggy Hutchison and John Lord. As her family, we continually grow in our understanding of the importance of inclusion and friendships to a good quality of life. We believe that Karen has a right to a good quality of life. We think this can only be achieved through an inclusive life. Inclusion means that Karen is included fully in her community, has the opportunity to grow to her fullest, has choice and self-determination, and is free from discrimination.

Karen with her extended family at the family cottage

Our daughter has always lived an inclusive life. As a child, she lived with us in a housing co-op that was participatory, where she was very involved in her neighbourhood. She attended a co-operative day care centre and public school with her siblings. Karen joined community activities, from Brownies to residential camp. These opportunities provided the foundation for beginning to live a full, inclusive life with relationships at the core.

As Karen grew to adulthood, her broad vocational interests, from day care teacher to cafe worker, contributed immensely to this full life. Living with people of her choice or on her own has been important to her becoming her own person. Making a contribution through singing in her church choir, playing in a community band, and working as a certified yoga instructor have all been central to her experiencing an inclusive life as a full citizen in the community of Kitchener-Waterloo, Ontario. Karen's immediate and extended family plays an active role in her life. Karen receives support from family and friends as well as from individualized funding that enables her to create her own path.

Friendships are central to this vision of inclusion. The power of friendship for belonging cannot be over-estimated. We know that friends and relationships are vital for self-esteem, dreams, participation, social support, and citizenship. Since Karen was a young child, we have intentionally worked on relationship building at every stage of her life. This has not always been easy but being aware of different approaches to building friendships has helped immensely with this process. We want to share with you what we have learned about friendship and the diverse approaches that can be used.

We do this by first an introduction to the topic. An introductory chapter will address why friendships are important, their connection to inclusion, and details about our personal experience. Next, five chapters outlining major approaches to friendship development, one for each approach to relationship building will follow. With each approach, we provide a definition; background and history according to the literature; strategies we have found important over the years as utilized with Karen; a summary of the potential of the approach, and a few resources for exploring these topics in greater depth. Detailed notes or references for each of these chapters appear at the end of the book. Finally, a concluding chapter draws conclusions by highlighting several themes that cross all five approaches to building relationships.

Finally, a word about the writing of this book is important here. This book is meant for people with disabilities, family members, and other people interested in building friendships within an inclusion framework. The intention of this book is not to offer a recipe to follow but rather to build interest in friendship as it relates to inclusion.

We got started with this idea based on some presentations we were doing. Over several years, Peggy and Karen developed and delivered a powerpoint presentation on these five approaches to building friendship that was shared with others. Karen understands the framework of inclusive friendships because she lives it. This has been presented in several places: Peggy's 4th year class on inclusion at Brock University; the Facilitation Leadership Group; Plan Lifetime Networks in Kitchener; a recent conference of the Canadian Association for Community Living in Toronto; and the "You've Gotta Have Friends" Conference in Langley, British Columbia.

Karen and Peggy presenting in Langley BC at the "You've Gotta Have Friends Conference"

Peggy Hutchison and John Lord raised the idea of turning presentation ideas and other experiences related to friendship into a book with Karen. Karen was thrilled. After each draft was written, Karen and Peggy went through the manuscript for Karen's feedback and agreement on what had been written. It was important to know that Karen felt she was fairly and accurately portrayed.

We then sent the book out to a few academic and non-academic reviewers. We want to thank Charlottle Dingwall, Theron Kramer, Krista Lord, Sarah Lord, Kathryn MacKay, Erin Sharpe, and Amber Zimmerman for their helpful comments on drafts of this book.

Introduction: Friends and Inclusion

Why Friends?

Friendships are an important aspect of all our lives. Immeasurable benefits result from having friends, depending on the meaning we attach to the concept and the depth of the relationships. Some widely agreed upon benefits of meaningful relationships include:[1]

§ providing companionship for people of all ages.

§ playing a role in identity development, autonomy, and self-esteem.

§ presenting peers who can have a positive influence.

§ experiencing social support.

§ playing a preventive role in health related issues

such as obesity, smoking, isolation or dementia.

§ creating a foundation for the development of romantic relationships.

§ being an important ingredient in the kind of world we want to create.

§ and establishing a part of being a valued citizen.

These broadly accepted benefits of friendships have not been applied to people with disabilities. This oversight is detrimental for meaningful inclusion and equality of persons with disabilities. Fortunately, some recent frameworks of disability have included the importance of relationships. Friendships are increasingly seen as vital to growth and development and personal well-being, whether in mental health, independent living, or community living movements.

Friends and Inclusion

The idea that friendship is an important part of building inclusive lives has been recognized for some time.[2] We want to build on the reasons already established and outlined on the importance of friendship. However, we want to re-look at friendship from the angle of the person with a disability.

Friends provide companionship for doing things in the community. Many people with disabilities associate mainly with their parents, other persons with disabilities, volunteers, or staff. These tendencies raise questions on the degree of inclusion experienced by people with disabilities. We know that having a broad group of friends opens doors to communities of people, enables people to overcome feelings of loneliness associated with isolation, and allows for more spontaneity. Taken together, these benefits make inclusion more possible.[3]

Closely related to the companionship idea, is the fact that friends can potentially enable people to venture out into the world. Friends provide security, confidence, and channels for trying out things in the community. Venturing out might feel frightening simply because of the unknown. Or it might seem intimidating if the person has been overprotected and been denied opportunities other people take for granted. Taking risks to try new things and doing this in a supported context are very important for building an inclusive life. Friendships have potential for helping to make this happen.[4]

Friends also help a person with a disability learn about him or herself. Many people need support in exploring questions that will build autonomy and an inclusive life in the community. Who am I? What are my dreams? How do I feel about myself? In large part, it is friends that make this kind of exploration possible, being role models and mentors, providing peer feedback, and placing value on the person's thoughts and dreams. Friends also have the opportunity to learn more about their own strengths. These kinds of interpersonal experiences increase acceptance of diversity in our communities and contributes to citizenship.[5]

Strong bonds of friendship is known to be a strong determinant of health. We are healthier when we have meaningful friendships and relationships in our lives. A recent summary of research on this question shows that "people's health depends on the quality of their social relationships."[6]

Finally, friends are important to building inclusive lives because they provide social support. This support may be practical around issues like transportation or finances. Or it might include moral support when a serious crisis arises in a person's life such as the support given by friends when someone becomes ill or dies.[7] Support is often ongoing and a two way street. When support goes both ways, the so-called receiver of support learns along the way and is able to return gifts in ways that are very meaningful for others.

Inclusive Settings

The importance of friendships has been explored within diverse community settings. One finding is that many children with disabilities who attend regular classrooms in their neighbourhood school benefit in many ways, one of which is friendships.[8] 'Regular' throughout this book means participation in generic community settings that are used by citizens without disabilities. Similarly, people in regular and supported employment find they are able to develop new friends with people without disabilities.[9] Children and adults, who are part of regular, inclusive community recreation, including inclusive camps, are more likely to make friends.[10]

In summary, we suggest that "Texture" be used as a metaphor for friendships in an inclusive life.[11] Like the texture in a beautiful fabric, people, in order to have full, inclusive lives require all the things we take for granted in a 'good life.' Like a good piece of cloth, people with disabilities require lots of intricately woven threads. People require meaningful relationships, connections to the community, and opportunities for participating and contributing.[12]

Our Experience

We have come to recognize five main approaches to building an inclusive life through friendships experienced in the life of our daughter Karen Lord. Karen was adopted into the Hutchison-Lord household at the age of 3 ½.

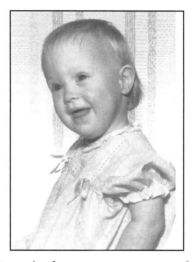

Karen's photo in newspaper column "Today's Child" – love at first sight!

Discussions about efforts to build friendships with Karen began during these early years together. Now an adult with a 'textured' life, this feels like the right time to reflect on the role of friendships in Karen's life and how they were facilitated.

Not coincidently, our commitment to inclusion began before Karen joined our family. We were already involved with teaching, research, and writing in the area of integration, as it was called in the late 70's, in opposition to segregation. Our first work together, as work and life partners, was a book called *Recreation Integration*, which became a foundation for our later work on inclusion.[13]   We furthered this work in the 80's and 90's through a community-based research organization we founded in Kitchener. The centre continues today with its focus on citizen participation, diversity, and inclusion. Peggy contributed during this time by bringing in her research from an academic context.

From the onset, it is important to emphasize that supporting Karen to build friendships and have an inclusive life has not been easy. Some readers may come to the conclusion that our ideas do not apply to a friend or someone they work with because the person does not have Karen's assets. Raising expectations has rewarding results.

It is true that Karen may seem like an exception today, but this was not always the case. The doctors told Karen's birth family that she was severely handicapped and they proceeded to give her up for adoption. We met Karen at 3 ½ in a foster home where she spent most of her time in a playpen, ate baby food, and was unable to walk or use the toilet. We were told that these were Karen's limitations. We were suspicious.

Our family treated Karen as a 3 ½ year old and not as a baby and from the onset began raising expectations and providing support for an inclusive life. We recognize that some people with disabilities have higher support needs, but we believe that

Karen with her new brother Jesse
and sister Krista

friendships are essential and possible for every person and enhance the lives of all, no matter what the severity of disability.

A final caution on a different note is needed here. In regards to the five approaches to friendship building, it is very easy for all of us to end up using each approach as a technique or tool. This can be a problem because a focus on tools can limit a broader understanding that is required to build friendships. One of the ways we have safeguarded this from happening has been to always have a goal for Karen's life in the forefront. A clear goal or better stated, a dream, can help us stay focused on 'community' and 'good process.' Our dream for Karen was and is to have the best possible quality of life and we have always strongly believed that this could only happen through an inclusive life of relationships.

Karen's thoughts on her own friendships in the quotations below reflect how her own dreams for friends have been fulfilled.

I have lots of friends.

I like friends who are outgoing.

I like friends who are good listeners.

My friends help me have a good life in the community.

I do lots of stuff with my friends like go to their house for dinner, do yoga together, drumming, go for coffee, and sharing with their kids.

I feel happy when I am with my friends. I feel joyful when I spend time with my close friends.

I like people and being with people. I talk with new people who are nice and friendly. And then sometimes we become friends.

Karen

Resources

Pahl, R. (2000). On friendship. Cambridge: Polity Press.

Amado, N. (Ed.). (1993). Friendships and community connections between people with and without developmental disabilities. Baltimore, MD: Paul Brookes Publishing.

Lord, J., & Hutchison, P. (2007). Pathways to inclusion: Building a new story with people and community. Toronto, ON: Captus Press.

Meyer, L., Park, H., Grenot-Scheyer, M., Schwartz, I., & Harry, B. (1998). Making friends: The influences of culture and development. Baltimore, MD: Paul Brookes Publishing Co.

Pedlar, A., Haworth, L., Hutchison, P., Taylor, A. & Dunn, P. (1999). A textured life: Empowerment and adults with developmental disabilities . Waterloo, ON: Laurier Press.

Staub, D. (1998). Delicate threads: Friendships between children with and without special needs in inclusive settings. Bethesda, MD: Woodbine House Inc.

Five Approaches
to Building Relationships

One to One

Social Networks

Circles

Bridging

Leisure Identities

Approach 1:
One-to-One

Several years ago, two young men were matched as part of a buddy program. For the first three months they got together every week. When the mandatory time for the match was completed, they decided to keep seeing each other. Now they see each other every couple of months to go to a hockey game and out for a beer.

Introduction

This story about two friends illustrates one of the most common ways that the one-to-one approach begins. A one-to-one approach refers to initiatives that offer one-to-one matches, normally between two individuals, but sometimes broader as we shall see. Often these are formal programs such as Peer Tutors, Best Buddies, Citizen Advocacy and Leisure Buddies. Alternatively, more informal arrangements can be made between two people. Frequently, these matches begin with the idea of one person helping another (like supporting a person to learn to read), leaving little possibility for friendship as there is a strong focus on an activity. In some approaches, the explicit purpose of the match is to foster a relationship or friendship.

Background

The concept of a one-to-one match for the purpose of friendship development as either a primary goal (friendship first) or secondary goal (friendship second) has been around for some time. For example, *Big Brothers/Big Sisters* has been in existence for over eighty years. Historically, it matched an adult to a young person who could benefit from an adult role model. The idea is that the adult provides support, mentoring, and friendship. Over 1,000 communities across Canada run these programs. In response to changing societal needs such as family breakdown, poverty, and youth-at-risk, new programs have been created such as "Couples for Kids," "Cross Gender Matching," "In-school Mentoring," "Big Bunch," and "Kids 'n' Kops".[1] The effectiveness of matching as a strategy and the mentoring process has been the subject of recent studies, which generally tend to show that the relationships formed play a very important role in people's lives.[2]

Peer Tutors are matches between students in the same grade or with a tutor in a higher grade. Studies suggest that advice from a peer is sometimes viewed more openly than from a teacher.[3] This program has been used with students with and without disabilities.[4] Similarly, *Reading Buddies* focuses only on reading literacy, and uses both 1:1 matches and small groups; often the mentor is a paid or unpaid staff.[5] Recently, a broader concept of peer support is emerging. This more inclusive approach helps ensure students with disabilities have full access to academic, social, and relationship opportunities.[6] Peer support, or peers helping each other, is a strong component of these initiatives.

Best Buddies International, Inc. (BBI) is a non-profit organization dedicated to enhancing the lives of people with intellectual disabilities by providing opportunities for one-to-one friendships and integrated employment. BBI now has partnered with more than 1400 college, high school, and middle school campuses internationally with accredited programs in six countries, including Canada. Basically, a country cannot begin a program without becoming an accredited program through BBI. Formal programs include Best Buddies Colleges (1989), Best Buddies

Citizens (1993), Best Buddies Jobs (1994), Best Buddies Highschools (1995), e-Buddies (1999), and Best Buddies Middle Schools (2000).[7] Best Buddies is vibrant in Canada.[8] It has been going for 15 years, has 200 chapters, and is the largest program internationally after the U.S. There has been a lot of research and writing about the Best Buddies program. These findings indicate a range of benefits from these programs, such as the development of friendships, access to regular employment, and positive attitudes towards persons with disabilities.[9]

Leisure Buddies is another one-to-one program for people with disabilities. This initiative has a lower profile since it operates informally, usually housed within larger organizations, unlike the earlier programs. Generally, volunteers are recruited to accompany a person with a disability to a recreation program.[10] Some community recreation departments across Canada offer this service.

Strategies for Making Things Happen in Karen's Life

With the five approaches to relationships, we discuss one-to-one strategies first because it was the one we were first aware of and the first one Karen experienced. An organization called *Extend a Family* supports family-to-individual matches in our community and we connected with this program in its infancy in the 1970's. In Karen's early years, we searched for an organization which promoted inclusion, because professionally we were involved in our community around integration issues as researchers. It was nearly impossible in those days to find initiatives practicing the philosophy we held deeply.

Extend a Family (EAF) is a non-profit organization committed to promoting the well being of individuals with a range of disabilities and their families. EAF takes a multi-layered approach involving partnership building, community development strategies, encouraging friendships, and generally promoting rights and inclusive communities. In addition to the family matching program, they provide other programs such as respite and *Best Buddies*.[11]

Our family became the first family match for this new organization even before Karen joined our family. We were matched to a family which included a child with a disability. The girl in their family was the same age as our eldest daughter and had the same name! This match lasted many years, and even today, the two girls, two grown women, see each other periodically.

When Karen was five years old we wanted this experience for her as well. We requested a family match from *Extend a Family* for our family for Karen. The purpose of our request was first and foremost friendship, although there is no doubt that over the years, it has provided some respite for us as parents. This match has been incredibly fruitful resulting in both friendship and a chance for Karen to learn and grow during her time with another family.

Our two families cultivated a family-to-family relationship. In the early years, Karen went to their home or their two girls would come to our place. They enjoyed playing together, sharing meals, sleep-overs, and watching movies. In these first few years, *Extend a Family* provided support in two ways. First, they would contact each of our families to see how things were going; and second, they had annual picnics that both families attended. Both of our families eventually had four children. As the years passed and we felt more secure in our relationship, we told *Extend a Family* their support was no longer needed. Attesting to the success of this match is the fact that 25 years later the girls are still fast friends.

*Karen with Extend-a-Family
friends Erin & Elizabeth*

*My friendship with the McHughs has been going
since I was a kid.*

*I used to sleep over when I was young. We went to
their grandparents house too who were really nice.*

I am friends with the whole family.

*They are good friends because they care about me.
I care about them.*

I see them all the time and they are nice.

*We do fun things together like going out to bars,
have dinner, or go out to movies.*

Karen

Karen with Extend-a-Family friends Erin & Elizabeth

Thinking back, there are a few reasons why this approach has worked well and produced lasting friendships. First, in our experience, the *values of the sponsoring organization* were instrumental to our success. Very few organizations have friendship building and inclusion as a core goal. The matching process from the beginning was designed around values and goals associated with inclusion. Second, the *matching and support process* was high quality and set the stage for developing friendships. The co-ordinator understood the importance of a sound process to the long term viability of the relationships in the match. She spent time getting to know both families and we even had a trial meeting before committing to the match. The follow-up support mentioned earlier was key to supporting the match over time. This support involved check-ins with the co-ordinator, conversations between parents, and occasional meals with both families. This entire process was also helped by the fact that both families are community minded, humanistic, and fun loving.

Third, the *parental factor* was key to the success of this approach. The McHugh family and especially the mother, Sharen, are guided by strong social justice values. She took on an organizer role ensuring regular visits happened, often every other week and never less than once a month. On top of this, Sharen made spontaneous check-in phone calls to our family. This woman's ability to 'weather' the strained and busy teen and college years by taking a flexible approach was important. For example, when their two girls seemed busy with schoolwork, Karen was still invited to join the family for dinners and socializing. As a result, Karen is now friends with all four of the children, all adults now, and the parents. What this story tells us is that it is essential that someone be a champion for relationship building.

Question to Sharen McHugh from Peggy:
As the relationship evolved between our two
families and especially between the girls, you
played a major role and continue to, in keeping the
relationship active. What motivated and inspired
you to do this? What do you think the benefits of
this matching process have been, now in its 25th
year, for Karen and for your family?

Response from Sharen McHugh: We wanted
our children to pick up by osmosis that personhood included everyone. Personhood in our
family would be defined by treating all persons
with dignity, respect, justice, and the right to
exist...We have all developed a comfort level and
the ability to see beyond the disabilities of others
to the individual. The benefit for both Karen and
our family is that Karen is viewed as a distinct
person and not a person with a disability.

Potential of the One-to-One Approach

There is one major weakness we experienced which
seems to be inherent in exclusive reliance upon the
one-to-one approach. Karen's friendships were mostly
limited to the matched family and their extended
family such as grandparents. This may have partly been
because the family was mostly home schooled and may

have had more limited contacts from which to expand relationships. More importantly, *Extend a Family* did not include a broader social network approach in its mandate and training.

A related weakness inherent in friendship in one-to-one programs is that the policies of many community organizations prohibit relationships continuing beyond the contract period. Many one-to-one programs emphasize spending time together and accompaniment to activities as their goals rather than building enduring friendship. Consequently, one-to-one set-ups often fall short on contributing to the social network of a person in the long term.[12]

Despite these shortcomings of the one-to-one approach, would we use it again? Absolutely! The beauty of the friendships emerging from one-to-one matches cannot be overshadowed by any problems we experienced. Had we defined the social networking concern earlier, we could have spent more time trying to adapt this approach. This became unnecessary, in a sense, because we discovered four other dynamic, complementary approaches that have served us well.

Resources

Best Buddies Canada www.bestbuddies.ca

Gillespie, P., & Lerner, N. (2000). The Allyn and Bacon Guide to Peer Tutoring. Needham Heights, MA: Allyn and Bacon.

Gold, D. (1988). A look at Leisure Buddy programs. In D. Gold & J. McGill, The pursuit of leisure. Toronto: G. Allan Roeher Institute.

Hutchison, P., & McGill, J. (1998). Leisure, integration, and community (2nd ed.). Toronto, ON: Leisurability Publications (p. 303).

Approach 2:
Social Networks

A teenage girl was somewhat isolated until her parents learned about social networks. Until then, she only went to school and did things with her family. With the assistance of a facilitator, this young woman and her family looked at her social network and consciously worked to build connections and relationships in each area of her network. Now she has joined an art class run at the community centre and a drop-in for youth at the Boys and Girls Club. She is volunteering after school now with seniors nearby her house. The family has also decided to re-connect with its church. In each of these settings, she has made new friends.

Introduction

This story about a girl who explored several community settings illustrates one way the social network approach often begins. The social network approach creates fertile ground for friendships by utilizing the various networks a person has in his or her life. Networks may be associated with one's neighbourhood, school, work, volunteering, family, faith community, and professional contacts. Social networks are very useful when we are trying to learn about new ways of relationship building.[1]

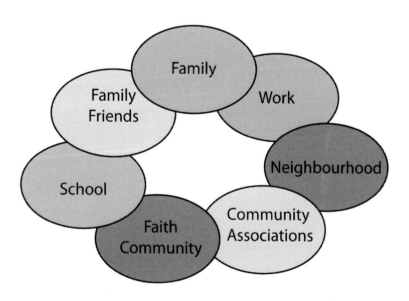

Some Examples of Social Networks

Background

Social network theory coming out of sociology says that the ties or relationships we have with others are critical and these ties can be understood by analyzing people's (or organization's) networks. Social network analysis provides a framework for making sense of the make-up and strength of a particular social network. Simply put, a social network can be viewed in the form of a map of all of our relevant ties. A visual of one's social network is useful in demonstrating connections between important things such as social support and friendship. [2] For example, when we analyze our own social networks, we may discover how certain people are more supportive than others or how others have the potential to become friends.

The social network approach has been used implicitly and explicitly as a mechanism for building friendships in specific settings. For example, neighbourhoods provide opportunities for children and families to build connections with other families in a variety of mutually supportive ways.[3] Neighbourhood schools may serve as a platform for building social networks and inclusion.[4] Inclusion efforts at schools emphasize the importance of strengthening relationships. [5] Employment may also provide an arena for social networks and friendship development.[6]

Finally, recreation and leisure provide an important context for developing social networks and friendships.[7]

Strategies for Making Things Happen in Karen's Life

As parents, we started using the social network approach to maximize inclusion and build friendships very early on. Using the social network approach encouraged us to think about the major areas of life like family, school, and work. We began to think about them in the context of inclusion, not disability. Consequently, inclusion became the 'dream' always at the forefront. This meant we would use 'regular' areas of life as our guideline for Karen's participation. Regular meant we would ask ourselves a few questions. Where do other people who don't have disabilities go? And what are the experiences of other people that could be of value to Karen?

When Karen first joined our family, our other children were attending a co-operative day care centre located at Peggy's place of work. We were certain that Karen going there would be a great opportunity for both her and our other kids. We might have kept her at home for awhile as John was a stay-at-home parent at that point, but we figured Karen could expand her social network through a day care experience. At the same time, we knew this idea of Karen attending a regular daycare was new thinking. This was not happening in many places, but it made complete sense in our minds. What better place to start learning about relationships than a co-op day care?

Eventually this 'regular' guideline meant Karen joined a regular class in our neighbourhood school, went to church, attended regular recreation and leisure programs, worked in everyday settings like day cares and Tim Horton's, and had regular roommates when

Karen in her church choir beside friends
Ruth and Julie

she started living apart from her parents. In all of these settings, the goal was established that Karen would be a full participant and contributor.

Anything done in Karen's life that was not regular or seemingly integrated would be an exception and done only for a very good reason. For example, over the years, Karen has been part of two self-advocacy groups, *People First* and *Opening New Doors*. While these self-help groups are comprised of people with disabilities, they are not considered to be segregated in the same way as many programs for labelled persons. Self-help is in a category of its own in that people join these groups on a volunteer basis. These have been excellent vehicles for Karen to learn about rights and to have a voice in disability issues that need to be addressed by the community. She has learned a great deal from other people with disabilities who have been self-advocates for many years before her time.

We also decided that 'regular' settings should be of good quality. In school, it was important that Karen receive the same curriculum as other children, from history to literacy, with necessary support. As parents, we taught her non-academic skills such as cooking, cleaning, and finances. To us, good quality also meant there were opportunities to work on social skills and relationships. We did not consider settings to be inclusive unless genuine friendships were nurtured and supported. An example of this type of support occurred when one of Karen's teachers shared stories with us about a real friendship that seemed to be starting. She raised the question of what the school and we could be doing to further encourage this, such as inviting the other child to our home.

Network Mapping

In the hope of enlarging Karen's networks, we have drawn upon MAPPING or a social network analysis. Mapping is an exercise for visualizing and analyzing social networks. Our experience tells us that this works best when a process is built intentionally, eventually becoming more natural. Following years of utilizing network analysis, we now approach all of Karen's networks with a 'relationship lens.' This allows us to search for possibilities and potential relationships and friendships in all community settings. In the early years, we as parents were co-ordinating her friendships, but in recent years, Karen has shown far more initiative related to nurturing and maintaining her own social networks. A facilitator now assists her with this process.

Specifically, we have used social networking as a tool in the following manner, but others may have discovered their own strategies. For each area of the network (integrated school, neighbourhood etc.) we take several steps.

§   We write down the names of all the people who the person has in his or her life in terms of depth of relationship: close friends, noteworthy relationships, and acquaintances.

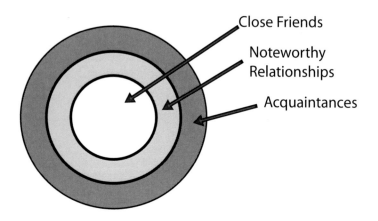

Close Friends

Noteworthy Relationships

Acquaintances

Depth of Relationships

§   For each name identified as a *close friend*, we indicate what is needed to ensure that the friendship continues, develops, and is supported, taking into account Karen's interest.

§   For each name identified as a *noteworthy relationship*, we identify reasons why this relationship may not have developed to a deeper level, whether we want to do anything about that, and if so, what might be a useful action?

§   At this point it can be valuable to do an overall assessment of the person's social network. In terms of each area of the person's life (e.g., work or school), we might evaluate the level of progress of real friendships and how are they contributing to an overall picture of an inclusive life. If the answer to this is less than satisfactory overall, or in one area, we might go back to the names of *acquaintances*. We might, for example, talk to acquaintances and see if they would be interested in being more involved in the person's life.

We have found this is a useful tool for mapping Karen's networks, but also have used this approach with other friends in Karen's network, to see how relationships can overlap and connect.

I make friends at work, at church, at school when I was a kid, and family friends.

I like having friends in all these different places. I have a very active life.

I like being in those places because people make me feel great.

They help me if I need help.

*Often we do things outside church or work like go
to parties at people's houses or have coffee.*

Karen

Sometimes a person's social network grows slowly
or hardly at all because there are too few areas of social
network involvement or too few that are inclusive.
In the case where a person has too few areas on his or
her map, for example only the neighbourhood and
family, adding more areas such as integrated work
or volunteering could be considered. For Karen, this
has seldom been an issue because she has been linked
into so many diverse communities and areas – such as
school, volunteering, employment, community
organizations, and church, resulting in many friends
and acquaintances.

Of course, this did not mean that everything was
smooth sailing. For example, it did take Karen a long
time to understand the reciprocal nature of friendship.
This continues to make friendship development a
challenge and has required perseverance on the part
of Karen's family and close friends. We can say that
hard work, creative energy, and strategic thinking are
important components of building strong social
networks.

Karen at work with friend Andrew

One thing that sometimes happens in social networks is the 'borrowing' from each other's networks. Many people do this from time to time: a friend invites another friend to a party, they meet each other's friends, and some of them become new friends. When Karen was younger, she often met and 'borrowed' friends from her sisters' networks of friends. Now Karen's networks are so rich and diverse that friends have borrowed from her networks!

Researchers and social activists are beginning to discover the power of networks and networking... These networks result from self-organization, where individuals

> recognize their interdependence and organize
> in ways that support the diversity and
> viability of all...The world changes...as
> networks of relationships form...[8]

Everyone might consider sharing their social
network or lending a friend if they knew someone
who needs a friend and think their friend is the kind
of person who would make a good friend for that
person. Both people are known well to us. Their
values, interests, and dreams could all assist in making
a connection by using the knowledge and experience
of each person in the transition period.

Karen with her friends Dave & Amanda
at their wedding

Potential of the Social Network Approach

It is possible that some people might see the social network approach as too complex. There are many areas to work on, such as school, family, and neighbourhood; there are many levels of friendship to consider, from good friends to acquaintances; and there are concepts like Mapping and social network analysis. Many people with disabilities we know have lives that already feel complicated.

Certainly we have found this approach to be more complex than most of the other approaches. Accountability to having real friends in each and every area of a person's life is no easy task. Yet there is richness in being able to *intentionally* identify and cultivate relationships in a number of networks. We have found that these network efforts pay off. This is an approach that has contributed significantly to Karen's and our quality of life, friendships, and inclusive lives.

Resources

Hutchison, P., & McGill, J. (1998). Leisure, integration, and community (2nd ed.). Toronto, ON: Leisurability Publications. p. 310.

Scott, J. Social network analysis: A handbook (2nd ed.). Thousand Oaks, CA: Sage Publications.

Stainback, W., & Stainback, S. (1990). Support networks for inclusive schooling: Interdependent integrated education. Baltimore, MD: Paul Brookes.

Approach 3: Circles

A man in his thirties has had a Circle now for many years. He was part of an organization that knew about Circles and helped him and his family start one. His Circle has always provided both support and friendship to him and his family. Now his Circle has six members and a few of the members have been with the Circle since the beginning. The Circle helps him with whatever he and the group decide are priorities. They have tackled everything from housing issues to nutrition, to his love life. Two of the people on the Circle are his very good friends and spend time with him regularly outside the Circle.

Introduction

This story about a man who has had a 'Circle' for many years exemplifies another important way friendships can be developed and supported. The concept of Circles is exactly as the term implies, a group of people circling the person. A Circle is a group of people who agree to meet, usually on a regular basis, to support a family member or friend. In many cases, the person can play an important role in inviting people to help him or her work on friendships, barriers, and dreams.[1]

Sometimes people distinguish between a 'Circle of Friends' and a 'Circle of Support,' depending on the focus of the Circle. Many times, both functions are provided and the group is simply called a 'Circle.' A third type of Circle is called a 'Microboard' that formally incorporates as a non-profit board with a legal mandate to handle funds and make decisions.[2] This is a more formalized arrangement, with the microboard serving as a legal 'board of directors' for the person's support arrangements and is used in cases where the person has individualized funding.

Background

Circles have mostly been used to provide support and build friendships for people with disabilities. Circles have also been used in a limited way to support older persons and persons who have offended.[3] The first influential work done with people with disabilities was *Circle of Friends* by Robert and Martha Perske and *What are we Learning about Circles of Support* by Beth Mount, Pat Beeman, and George Ducharme, both in 1988.[4] In 1991, Jack Pearpoint wrote about the Circle of friends around his friend, Judith Snow, who had been living in a chronic care hospital. This was the first recorded Circle in Canada.[5] Judith's Circle of friends helped her become an international leader who now teaches and writes about labelling, friendship, and inclusion. A few publications of a more practical nature followed this early work, including 'how to's' for people wanting to actually put this approach into action.[6]

There is a growing body of research from the last twenty years that has increased our knowledge of the process and demonstrated the impact of Circles, including more support for families and improved relationships.[7]

Strategies for Making Things Happen in Karen's Life

We first started a Circle with Karen when she was in grade five. The reason for pursuing this emerged out of a particular context. At age ten we moved Karen to the Catholic Board in our area that had a new Director of Education known for his leadership around inclusion. The Public Board had put up considerable resistance to the practice of inclusion. Karen's transition to a new school system seemed like a good time to start a Circle. First, the new board encouraged Circles and went as far as hiring Marsha Forest as an integration consultant for several schools. Her role was to educate and support principals and teachers as well as facilitate the development of Circles. Second, we thought that it might help Karen make new friends during her transition to a new school and board. Third, at about the same time we visited our friend and colleague, Judith Snow, who we had known since the early 80's. She asked us in her usual direct way, "Does Karen have a Circle yet?" We responded "No, we weren't sure we needed one." Insightful as usual, Judith said: "It's not about need; it's about a life with relationships." Judith is an expert on the power of Circles. Her knowledge and own personal experience was to be taken seriously.

Karen's Circle meeting

The *make-up* of a Circle is always worth examining. Karen's original Circle constituted parents, siblings, and a few classmates. It functioned more like a Circle of friends. Later the focus of the Circle broadened to include both friendship and support. It now looks more like a Circle of support and decision-making in addition to friendship. Meetings take place at our home with several members staying constant over the years, such as parents, siblings, and a few close friends like the McHugh family. Selected friends have been added along the way, especially individuals who seem quite 'bonded' to Karen and have expressed an interest in her future well being. Karen makes final decisions on Circle recruitment, with consultation with others.

Originally, the Circle met several times a year, but now it meets once or twice a year.

We initially placed a high degree of importance on the role of facilitation in the Circle. The school's integration consultant facilitated the first Circle meetings held at the school. Karen's Circle initially created a MAP (originally Making Action Plans), which is a planning tool with eight steps.[8] Our hope that this planning process would strengthen existing friendships and produce new ones was realized. One friend from Karen's class started coming to our house most mornings, eating breakfast, and walking with Karen to school. Our entire family recently attended his wedding.

Sometimes family members have facilitated our Circle gatherings, while other times, a staff person supporting Karen with building relationships and connections plays this role. In our experience, without good facilitation, it is difficult for Circles to stay focussed and action-oriented.

We also learned along the way that it is important for a Circle to find ways to *rejuvenate*. One of many ways we did this was when Karen was around age 16 we did a PATH, a well recognized planning approach,[9] as a way of bringing in several new members. These new members included a friend of Karen's from church, a friend from work who is now a stay-at-home mom with three children who Karen loves, an adult couple who is friends of Karen's parents, and a favourite relative. Sometimes we evaluate a certain Circle member's participation and gradually support them to phase out if they have other pressing priorities to which they must attend.

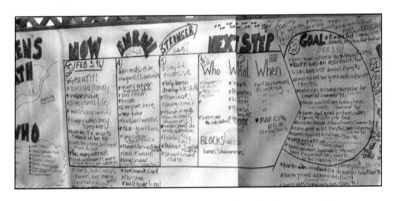

Karen's PATH, created with her Circle

It is also important to think about the various roles Circle members play. First and foremost is the role of Karen, who can be considered the focus person. Karen has always been involved with planning the agenda of meetings, co-running the meetings, as well as contacting and connecting with members outside meetings. Her role developed, gradually into being more leadership-oriented. Consequently, as Karen has built her own capacity, the role of other members has adjusted accordingly.

The role of our family could be described as a tightrope: on one hand providing energy and leadership to the Circle; on the other hand, backing off when Karen or her friends hint we are doing too much or when we are interfering with her or their roles.

The role of each member is vital to the long term viability of the Circle. We have found that members who only attend meetings and have failed to establish a clear role and relationship outside Circle meetings usually end up leaving. Circle members occasionally break into groups of twos or threes to work on issues with Karen between meetings. For example, a few years ago, Karen wanted to leave her work in daycare after ten years. A few Circle members spent many hours supporting her and developing action steps towards obtaining new employment.

I have a Circle.

I have friends on my Circle. My sisters Krista and Sarah are on my Circle as well as friends.

At meetings we talk, plan, sometimes do a MAP, and we celebrate by eating meals. They help me figure things out like moving away from home and finding a new job.

I do things with each person. Like my Aunt Ann and Uncle Peter, I take the train or bus to London and stay for the weekend.

I trust my Circle members. I have dreams and goals and my Circle helps me with these.

Karen

We have found as a Circle that it has been very important to learn how to be strategic. This has been especially imperative around transition times like ending high school, moving away from home, boredom with a current job, or finding a life partner. Being strategic makes a difference because supporting Karen to build and experience an inclusive life with friendships is faced with challenges. For example, the Circle has long been hearing about Karen's dream for a boyfriend. A variety of strategies have been explored including on-line dating, attending the Down Syndrome Society AGM party, passing the word on to everyone we know, and keeping parents out of the match-matching business. This reminds us that while the focus of Karen's Circle is on her, it is also about setting principles and strategies for the whole family. "It takes a village" is a good metaphor for the Circle and building an inclusive life with Karen.

Another way that Karen's Circle is strategic is that we try to be *intentional* about the strengths and community connections we all bring to the Circle. For example, we often encourage connections between Karen and a Circle member if we know they share a common interest. This also builds on the concept of 'borrowing' networks discussed earlier.

§ *Karen has several members of her Circle*

§ *Karen visits each of them regularly*

§ *Each of these persons has his or her own life, interests, and relationships separate from Karen*

§ *When Karen visits, there is potential for her to benefit from this by tapping into their lives, sharing their interests, and connecting with their friends*

The Process of Relationship Development with a Circle

Potential of the Circle Approach

Like the one-to-one approach, the 'Circle' can be limited if relied upon as the only approach because of its structure. Relationship development seldom goes beyond Circle members. Occasionally, Karen does connect with the network of another Circle member. Although this only happens to a certain degree with Karen's Circle, it is a minor concern since the Circle approach is always used in conjunction with other approaches.

Additionally, Circles may experience challenges related to the long term commitment required of members. While turn-over brings fresh blood and energy, it also makes continuity difficult. The consequence is that existing members must assume a heavier load. Additionally, if a Circle is too small, the energy and skill needed in a Circle may be limited.

It is a problem when people use the Circle concept in a limited way. For example, a Circle may become more about managing and strengthening support services (i.e. staffing), than relationship building and community connecting. It takes a strong commitment, and often a champion, to keep a Circle active and focussed on relationships and friendships.

Despite shortcomings, the Circle has been an excellent approach for Karen. The very word 'Circle' in Karen's mind conjures up images of a colourful visual that includes working on rights, acting on dreams, planning life changes, and enjoying celebrations.

Resources

Falvey, M., Forest, M., Pearpoint, J., & Rosenberg, R. (1997). All my life's a Circle: Using the tools: Circles, MAPS & PATHS. Toronto: Inclusion Press.

Mount, B., Beeman, P., & Ducharme, G. (1988). What are we learning about Circles of support? Connecticut: Communitas.

Pearpoint, J. (1991). From behind the piano: The building of Judith Snow's unique Circle of friends. Toronto: Inclusion Press.

Perske, R., & Perske, M. (1988). Circle of friends: People with disabilities and their friends enrich the lives of one another. Burlington, ON: Welsh Publishing Co.

Approach 4:

Bridging

A young woman grew up in a family that loved all the great symphonies. She loved music as well. Whenever possible she listened to classical music. Her neighbour had tickets to the local symphony orchestra and invited her to attend from time to time. After one concert, she asked the conductor if she could attend rehearsals. She became a regular at symphony rehearsals, and soon after became a volunteer with the symphony. Over time, she developed relationships with fellow volunteers, one of whom owned a coffee shop in her neighbourhood. Soon she was a regular at the coffee shop. It was there that she met her boyfriend.

Introduction

This story about a woman with a lifelong love for music illustrates the beauty of the bridging approach for developing friends. The bridging approach to building relationships is about connecting with more informal places, spaces, and organizations in our communities. It is based on the belief that it is in these more informal places that relationships can be nurtured.[1] Sometimes this approach is known as 'associational.'

Bridging is especially important for citizens with disabilities because research shows that many people with disabilities spend the majority of their time in separate places specifically designed for persons with disabilities, rather than experiencing full citizenship in our communities.[2] Bridging enables people to experience participation and contribution in community, the essence of citizenship.

Background

Robert Putnam in his books *Bowling Alone* and *Better Together* argues that North American societies have gradually become more disconnected from family and friends and democratic structures. According to

Putnam, our society has undergone a decline in civic, associational, civil, political, and social life.[3] He says that this is because our world has become more and more suburbanized, individualized, specialized, professionalized, and fast-paced. Many people now believe that we need to re-discover community as part of a broad strategy for more cohesive and simpler times.[4] Relationship building through participation in more informal places makes sense.

The process of bridging usually begins with an understanding of the person's strengths, gifts, and interests. If we know that Joe Smith has an interest in books or science, it gives us a starting point for connecting him with some aspect of his community. A 'bridger' typically sees two distinct pathways to community that might be considered informal. They are both described below. These two places afford plentiful opportunities for informal relationship building.

§ *Everyday public spaces:* parks and coffee shops, as well as events such as festivals; researchers sometimes refer to these as 'third' places because they provide informal space for conversation and connection.[5]

§ *Community associations:* faith communities, clubs, and community centres; these are also known as places of common interest.

Community members who are marginalized due to a disability can become involved in various places in the community by a connection based on a common interest. A strengths or asset based approach (in contrast to a deficit approach) is used by bridgers assisting people previously not seen as contributors to community building. We find the process of connecting people with informal settings can increase the community's ability to become more hospitable.[6] Once people are included in community spaces and organizations, opportunities may arise for friendships to develop.

Many practical guides have been published that are filled with strategies and resources associated with the bridging approach.[7] The experience from one community emphasizes the importance of starting small, for example, with one person, leader, neighbour, neigbhourhood organization, or project.[8] Another guide called 101 Ways to Make Friends by Aaron Johannes & Susan Kurliak outlines many ways that relate to connecting such as: # 7 Make a community inventory: map your neighbourhood and the opportunities that are there; #21 Support your local amateur sports teams; #30 Join a spiritual gathering place; #40 Go to the local pub to watch the game (instead of watching it at home alone); #47 Take a class at the local community centre; #69 Shop locally; and #99 See yourself as a community builder.[9]

John McKnight, whose name is synonymous with the bridging/associational approach, has been researching, writing, and advocating over the past twenty years in regards to life beyond services. While several practical guides use the asset-based approach, here is one of McKnight's thoughts about gifts, which are one foundation to relationship building:

> ...the "giftedness" of every individual is particularly important to apply to persons who often find themselves marginalized by communities. It is essential to recognize the capacities of those who have been labelled mentally handicapped or disabled... In a community where assets are being fully recognized and mobilized, these people too will be part of the action, not as clients or recipients of aid, but as full contributors to the community-building process. [10]

Strategies for Making Things Happen in Karen's Life

We first became aware of and involved with bridging or the associational approach when Karen was very young. As parents, we were aware of the importance of recreation and leisure opportunities because of our backgrounds and experience. Accordingly, we got Karen involved with a range of community groups. She joined the Girl Guide movement at age 6 (Sparks, Brownies, Guides), played baseball and soccer through the local Parks and Recreation, took art classes, and later took advantage of karate, tai chi, and yoga classes that were offered by

Karen with her Brownie friends at Guide camp

a variety of community associations. We also joined a local community church.

When Karen was a child, we made many of these decisions about community participation for her, as with our other children. However, as Karen got older and gained experience, she began to sort out her own preferences for community activities. For example, our love of the out-of-doors and long history with camping meant we encouraged our children to try this. Karen decided that residential camp was a definite yes and baseball was a definite NO. She attended summer camps with her siblings starting at age 8.

While Karen was integrated in all of these activities, we never assumed that she was experiencing full inclusion. We discovered that there was often an additional process that was needed to ensure opportunities were inclusive. We would usually meet with leaders to give them insights into Karen's dreams, her gifts, our expectations, and the importance of communicating with us to keep things on track. This process was similar for everything she got involved in. However, the content would vary depending on the context. For example, preparation for residential camp was different than preparation for joining an art class.

Ricki, a camp friend originally, is an artist and bakery owner in Pelee Island, where Karen visits annually; Ricki and Karen were also roommates for several years

When preparing Karen for camp, we might complete a detailed application form, meet months ahead with an inclusion specialist, and visit the camp on the first day. We would then meet the director and inclusion specialist to finalize supports and expectations and emphasize Karen's gifts, meet the camp nurse, and remind Karen of her responsibilities in addition to having fun. When we picked her up, we would once again meet with staff and discuss how things went and try to find out about friendships that started that could be continued during the year.

If Karen were taking an art class, we would meet with the teacher sometimes ahead of time to make sure the philosophy of the teacher regarding art and teaching was consistent with our beliefs. Furthermore, we would discuss inclusion strategies such as the use of co-participants providing support and nurturing friendship. Depending on our assessment of the program, we might keep an eye on it to ensure things were developing nicely. If no friendships were forming, we would seriously examine the situation and decide whether or not this was an adequate or suitable environment for future years.

At church, Karen has been involved in a variety of roles as a member, from choir member to drummer during services over the years. While family supported her initially, eventually everyone at church came to know Karen, she came to know them, and most importantly, several close friendships emerged from her church involvement. She has taken on valued roles in church related activities and participated and contributed to church life. Her church friends share her love of music, attend concerts, and have dinners together.

The Girl Guide experience lasted many years because the leader became friends with Karen and invited her to be a co-leader for younger groups. This was a rich and meaningful experience. An opportunity related to this experience is that participants can stay involved with the Guide Movement for years, making friendships more possible. Karen's bottom line is that friendships and relationships (not just skills and presence) had to evolve out of her participation or she lost interest, as did we as parents.

Karen continues to go to overnight summer camp because, as with the Girl Guide leader, selected camp directors understand the importance of people with disabilities having valued roles. As an adult, she is invited yearly to join the staff on a part-time basis and now teaches art, yoga, and is a song leader. These experiences are satisfying for immeasurable reasons but the friendships are why she returns year after year. Camp is grounded in a community oriented perspective and has a partnership with a provincial camp inclusion support initiative (Project Rainbow). Initially, Rainbow supported Karen's inclusion but has since stepped away from the role due to the success.

With bridging strategies, we have found that in most cases, greater support is needed at the beginning of an activity and during transitions. Wherever possible, these supports are gradually withdrawn as Karen becomes more confident and involved. Another lesson is that support may come from various and sometimes unexpected sources, including ourselves as parents, the leader, co-participants, or friends. Over the years, we as parents have spent considerable time nurturing and encouraging supportive relationships.

As an adult, informal settings are very important for Karen. They are places where hospitality and relationships thrive. They are places for conversation and connection.

Sometimes I like just hanging out like at the cafe.

Sometimes people come by and we chat. I like having coffee with friends.

I like coffee hour after church where we just stay around and talk and gossip.

Our church has small groups that meet in people's homes and we talk and eat.

At camp after our campers are asleep the staff talk, hang out, eat, and watch movies.

I write my friends on facebook.

Karen

Potental of the Bridging Approach

Over the years, Karen's participation in community associations and activities has not always led to friendships. In particular, time-limited short term programs like swimming classes usually yield no friends. Inviting a friend to attend a regular program with Karen has made relationship building more feasible. When programs she was attending were ongoing from year to year, it was worth the investment to help the leaders of the program understand inclusion. One time we picked Karen up from camp and discovered she spent the entire week on a counsellor-in-training's knee rather than being with peers. Over time, we have found that relationships do not develop in inclusive settings unless people in those settings are intentional about helping Karen build supportive relationships. Of course, all of this takes time and energy to keep people informed about inclusion.

Bridging can lead to citizenship because it enhances people's participation and contribution. Yet if bridging is to lead to relationship development, the process must pay attention to what actually happens within informal settings. We have found that identifying a 'connector' within the setting can be an asset. Sometimes this is a group leader, while often it is a peer who shows interest in Karen and seems to be connected with her in some way.

Bridging as an approach to building an inclusive life has been vital over the years for Karen. It has produced friendships that lead to everything from roommates, to jobs, companionship, and skills development. This approach was and still is beneficial because the informal and self-directed nature of Karen's involvements make it possible to focus on her gifts, support her in making a contribution, and nurture lifelong friends.

§ *Natural connectors*

§ *Diversity valued*

§ *Relationships valued over skills and activities*

§ *Hospitality intrinsic*

§ *Asset based*

§ *Informal and unstructured*

§ *Leaders find ways to involve everyone*

Characteristics of Welcoming Settings
Inherent in Bridging

Friends & Inclusion

Approach 5:
Leisure Identities

A woman has always been interested in baseball. When she was a child she would watch her older brother's games. Her parents signed her up for girl's baseball when she was eight. Her skills lagged behind other girls her age but she persisted. It was a small town and she became friends with everyone on the team. Eventually the coach of the team spoke to her parents who agreed with the coach's suggestion that she practice with the team, and be the assistant coach during games. Everyone around town knows what a good player she is, how much she loves baseball, and how dedicated a coach she is. Recently she was invited to be a co-coach with the girl's junior team and she accepted the position.

Introduction

This story about a woman who had a passion for baseball illustrates the power of the leisure identity approach for making friends, as well as gaining a valued role in community. 'Leisure identities' is an approach that uses a strong interest in a leisure activity (e.g., skiing, chess) to strengthen personal identity. When a person shows a passionate interest in something, parents or friends can encourage the person to pursue it more deeply by supporting him or her with everything from encouragement, to driving and financial help. Eventually, after years of the person focusing, persisting, and taking the activity seriously, others who know the person, such as family, friends, or community members, see the person as more than 'he likes skiing' but instead 'he is a skier,' or 'his life is skiing.' They come to strongly associate this interest with the person and hence a leisure identity. This intense participation is supported by the person and others because it is acknowledged as a strong contributor to identity formation and self-esteem. This powerful process can also be harnessed as a vehicle for relationship building.

Background

Parents have long recognized the emotional, social, and physical benefits their children gain from intense participation in a leisure activity. Based on the belief that participation is linked to everything from academic performance to choice of peers, many parents support the involvement of their children in both formal and informal school and community activities.[1]

Over the years, discussions about the idea of *'serious leisure'* have also contributed to our understanding of leisure identities. Robert Stebbins' pioneering work, beginning in the early 70's, looked at leisure activities and the role of leisure in identity formation. Serious leisure is the pursuit of an amateur, hobbyist, or volunteer activity. 'Serious' embodies concepts such as earnestness, sincerity, importance, carefulness, and commitment.[2] Since then, the concept has provided the theoretical framework for studying everything from quilters to sport fans.[3] Additionally the concept has been applied to lifespan issues such as youth development and successful aging for seniors.[4]

There have been diverse benefits of serious leisure documented over the years; however, of particular interest to us as parents, is the social nature embodied in this concept. For example, rewards come in the form of meeting people, making new friends, and having in-depth conversations with people sharing a similar interest.[5]

The concept has also been applied to a limited degree with vulnerable persons, such as persons with disabilities.[6] The most comprehensive work on this subject is *Developing Leisure Identities* by Judith McGill.[7] Essentially this approach is used not only to strengthen a person's identity, but to build relationships at the same time. This is done by the person getting involved in an activity in which he or she has a very strong interest. The person is supported (e.g., financially, emotionally, physically) to do this activity in an intense way. Through this intense participation, often over many years, the person strengthens his or her identity in one of two ways (or both): through acquiring skills associated with participation in this activity; and through forming relationships and making friends with people who have similar interests.

Strategies for Making Things Happen in Karen's Life

Since Karen was a child, we were aware that supporting all four of our children to be involved in community activities was very important in terms of health and fitness, socialization, and generally having

As you can see from this picture, Karen let us know whether she liked or disliked something...

a good quality life. As with all our children, we would watch for what Karen would 'take to' and encourage her to pursue things she had an aptitude for and an interest in. Like some children, she was never drawn to competitive activities, but rather was more interested in the arts: music, movement, drama, and fine arts.

Drumming Identity

One activity that could be considered a leisure identity for Karen is drumming. Karen was always interested in music and singing but we weren't able to find an instrument that worked for her...until the drum. A friend actually got Karen started. When Karen went to her house to hang out, do yoga, or spend time with her children, Karen started playing her drum. The friend noticed how fast she established a beat and how much joy it brought to her.

*Karen drumming with friends at the
Waterloo Community Band*

Over the years, Karen has expanded her interest in drumming. She has taken lessons, bought a drum kit, performs regularly at church with an accompanist on the bongo or cello, is a member of a drumming circle that meets in the park in the summer and an indoor arts centre in the winter, attends an annual women's drum camp weekend, and is one of two drummers in the local community band.

In all of these drumming pursuits, Karen sometimes goes with a friend and always builds relationships there. Many of the people who have the 'drum identity' are interested in a sense of community. So people start with their love of drumming but often talk about other things that are important to them such as community events and other concerts.

Drumming at house party with friends Glen and Phil

Yoga Identity

Another activity that Karen showed interest in was karate. For many years, she worked hard at this discipline, earning her green belt. Karate gave her fitness and confidence. We had noticed that there were a few people in this club who were very supportive of Karen, but no real friendships developed. Eventually she wanted a change. By this time we were guided by the idea that presence and participation is not enough unless relationships follow.

Yoga was her next choice. Around age 20, Karen made a friend who was into yoga in a big way; they did a bit of yoga at home together and she encouraged Karen to join a yoga club that met weekly. Since then,

Karen with Yoga friends

Karen has been involved in several yoga clubs. Some friendships have come out of these groups. Sometimes a relationship will get started by something as simple as Karen asking for a ride home. One time a friend asked Karen to join a different club than the one that she was attending. More recently, Karen volunteered as an assistant instructor at a club that offers programs mostly for children.

This yoga experience sparked Karen's interest in studying to be a yoga instructor herself. She first expressed this 'dream' quietly to her family and friends.

A woman who is a facilitator with Karen began to explore yoga options in the community with Karen. They approached a yoga club to inquire about teacher training and the director was supportive. Karen signed up for an intensive one year yoga teacher program. For her, this meant committing to weekly sessions, week-end workshops, and exams.

Given the intensity of the program, together the director and Karen decided to spread the course over one and a half years. The director also gave a free teacher training voucher to another person who wanted to teach yoga and could volunteer to support Karen. This woman came to Karen's place once a week to review the class work with her. Karen now knows

Karen, certified yoga instructor, with one of her classes

every muscle and bone by their names, is extremely fit, is learning about teaching people of different ages, and knows all the ins and outs of how to teach each yoga position. Now a certified yoga graduate, Karen is now teaching yoga at people's work places. She also runs a yoga group at the camp she works at in the summer. Karen is a good leader, with lots of enthusiasm and confidence.

Just as important, several of the women who have been taking the yoga teaching course have become friends. Many of the people who have a 'yoga identity' also have other shared interests and values– they are into good nutrition, an active lifestyle, saving 'mother earth,' and building a sense of community in their lives through this strong leisure interest. This leisure identity has greatly strengthened Karen's relationship network.

I love yoga. I feel like a yoga queen.

I wanted to be a yoga teacher and now I am.

Training is very intensive but I love it. I learned the muscle names, like the rhomboids, gluteus maximus and bones.

We learned all the poses like the mountain, tree, downward facing dog, and forward bend. I learned to teach.

I like teaching. I never get nervous. It feels awesome to be a yoga teacher.

I have good relationships with other yoga people.

Karen

Travel

A third area that we must mention, albeit briefly, is the area of travel. Since Karen was a child in our family, she has had the privilege of being able to travel. Karen has been many places and loves to visit family and friends. As a child she visited New York to stay with her great Aunt. Relatives also live in Vancouver and South Carolina. Karen's aunt and uncle live in London, Ontario and Karen frequently takes the train and is developing a network of friends there. She has been to Mexico. She has also been to Germany to visit a friend. Many of her friends are currently living in places like Great Britain and Nova Scotia so she is plotting to visit them, not simply content with 'Skype' and a webcam.' She recently visited London, England to visit her friend Julie. Karen's experiences with travel are an important way she shares with her friends, and contributes to her being an interesting friend. For her friends at home who travel, this shared leisure identity provide a common ground for discussion.

*Karen with friends Meghan and Kristi
at their wedding in Nova Scotia*

Potential of the Leisure Identities Approach

The 'leisure identity' approach has not been without its challenges. Whenever Karen has attended a community activity, we have had to be aware of the importance of friendships. Since we have never attended programs or activities with Karen, we have had to depend on others to facilitate relationships. Leaders or co-participants who are aware of inclusion and the social aspects of these programs or activities can play a key facilitation role. Some people intuitively do that, and others don't. Fortunately, as Karen has gotten older, she has built on her life experience and she is now more interested in meeting people and making friends. She knows whether people are being patronizing or are genuinely interested in being a friend.

This approach has been most useful over the years in terms of Karen getting intensely involved in a few activities, building skills, acquiring friends, and making a contribution to her community. Karen's passions have been realized. This has contributed to living a more inclusive life. Karen is just another group member wanting to drum and do yoga and make friends.

§ *The person has an interest in something like an activity, sport, or hobby*

§ *The person connects with others with that interest*

§ *The person increases his or her commitment and deepens skills and involvement*

§ *Relationships are made in the process with others who share this interest*

§ *Friendships gradually evolve from those relationships*

The Leisure Identity Process Experienced by Karen and Others

Resources

McGill, J. (1996). Developing leisure identities: A pilot project. Brampton, ON: Brampton Caledon Community Living

Stebbins, R. (2006). Serious leisure: A perspective for our time. Piscataway: NJ: Transaction Publishers.

Conclusion:

Relationships Make a Difference

Introduction

We began this book by looking at the importance of friendship for everyone. We explored the meaning and history of five approaches to building relationships. Finally, we outlined how each approach was used in the life of Karen Lord, including some constraints and conclusions about the value of each approach.

In this final section, we outline broad themes that cross all five approaches: intentionality; self-determination; relationship lens; community as a first resort; depth of relationships; facilitation; and finally, sustainability. These themes all illustrate the power of thinking about friendship in this comprehensive way. It is hoped that this reflection will shed further light on the usefulness of these approaches individually and collectively.

Intentionality

> You gotta want to change. We mean want to change, desire it... to change, we intend change. Intention is the result of a decision (free will) to change, and that decision arises out of a desire to change.[1]

Intentionality is about planning and being deliberate. It is a very important part of the relationship building process.[2] There are several ways we have been intentional about relationships with Karen. First, we have educated ourselves and Karen about the different approaches, and the particular ways each approach can be used, including its strengths and weaknesses. This has enabled us to make wise choices about when and where to use each approach, and how to focus our energy.

We are intentional about when in Karen's life we need to be more careful around planning and facilitating friendship development. For example, during transitions in her life (i.e., finishing high school, starting a new job, friends moving away), when she might have been vulnerable to losing friends, we tried our best to make sure old friendships were maintained and new friendships nurtured.

An important part of intentionality is the ability to ask. This might mean asking someone if he or she is interested in being a one-to-one family with Karen, joining Karen's circle, or attending a weekend drumming camp. During times when we didn't know who or how to ask, we needed to find someone in our network that was better at asking. For example, Karen's older sister is an excellent network builder. She often enabled Karen to 'borrow' from her network by asking her friends to include Karen in their activities. Sometimes we need to be intentional in order to build opportunity, practice, and experience with relationships.

Self-Determination

Self-determination is important to friendship building.[3] Self-determination is about a person having choice or freedom to act on one's own and have control over his or her own life. Building friendships within an inclusive paradigm, regardless of the approach, cannot happen without self-determination.

For Karen, and her friends and family, self-determination has been a process that has been learned over many years. Self-determination provides the foundation for all five approaches to building friendship. No action around friendship building takes place without the participation of Karen.

However, self-determination may have different faces depending on which approach to friendship is being used. For example, one way self-determination happened with Karen's one-to-one family in earlier years was that Karen made it clear that this family was HER friends. Regardless of the approach that is being used, Karen is asked by her family and friends to continually make choices about what she wants to do and with whom. This is not always easy, as Karen is a busy person and sometimes double-books; like many of us, she has had to learn that self-determination is balanced with our interactions with others. Now she is obliged to the friend to whom she has made the first commitment. Karen is learning that self-determination operates within the context of other people and community.

Relationship Lens

Another important theme in all five approaches is the idea of a 'relationship lens.' The idea of a lens has been used as a metaphor by others.[4] What we mean when we use it here is that a 'relationship lens' is always at the forefront when we are working on inclusion. We are always looking for the potential for relationships in everything Karen does.

For example, Karen might be trying to find a new job or attend a yoga course, but possibilities for relationship building are always being noticed. Utilizing a relationship lens might also influence which approach(es) to friendship building we choose. Attending the yoga course would bring to mind 'leisure identities' because of her strong interest in yoga; or perhaps 'bridging' because of its potential for building relationships in more informal associations, or both.

But once participating, the 'relationship lens' would also encourage us to be looking at the world in terms of relationships and asking questions such as what relationships currently exist? Or does the potential exist for relationship development? Or who could we invite to participate? We would look for connections and notice relationships that exist between other people and think about how we might be able to tap into those existing relationships. And we would be noticing ways that connections and relationships can be nurtured or strengthened.

Community as a First Resort

'Community as a first resort' is similar to the lens theme in that community is always our first choice when building friendships no matter what approach we are considering. By community, we mean using all the regular places that are inhabited by all citizens, such as neighbourhoods, restaurants, places of worship, and cultural festivals.[5] It is in these regular places that more vulnerable citizens have the potential for making friends. Many people with labels have lives that are too structured or formal for friendship building to really take a hold.

The use of our five approaches to building friendship has made it possible for Karen to be *in* the community, not just *of* the community. Each of these approaches is used to promote inclusion. Regular preschool, school, classrooms, community associations, and work places have been Karen's life. Finally, Karen is involved in some programs which are mostly small informal organizations like clubs or groups. Karen spends much of her time with friends in more informal ways like 'pubbing,' sharing meals at friends' houses, chatting it up on the phone, and watching movies.

Depth of Relationships

In all of our approaches to building friendships the issue of depth of relationship is a theme. This issue has also been evident in some of the literature. Terminology such as 'just' friends, 'good' friends, 'best' friends and others are explored.[6] In the relationship map below we note that not all relationships will be the same in terms of intensity. Relationships range from acquaintance to close friend to intimate. We have learned that it is important not to judge the different types of relationships and to understand the strengths

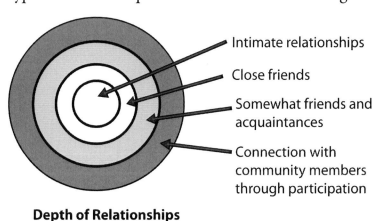

Intimate relationships

Close friends

Somewhat friends and acquaintances

Connection with community members through participation

Depth of Relationships

of each. For example, in Karen's life, there has been many benefits associated with weak ties or people who have been community members or acquaintances. This insight about depth of relationship would apply whether we are using a 'social network,' 'Circle,' or 'bridging' approach.

There are many questions about friendship that we have asked over the years pertaining specifically to Karen, but in fact, all of us probably wonder about these questions. What is a good friend? How many good friends does someone need? Is someone just an acquaintance or are they a friend? Does the person like me as much as I like them? How could we get to be better friends? And for Karen, a key question is "how much do *I* like someone?"

Facilitation

Facilitation has been important to all approaches to friendship building for Karen. In our context, facilitation is a term used to describe a way to support vulnerable persons that is about enabling, self-determination, inclusion, and building welcoming communities.[7] Facilitation is documented in the literature as a mechanism for building friendships within inclusive settings. [8]

Relationship building is an essential part of the work of facilitators. It is through relationships that people with disabilities experience the richness and diversity that community has to offer. Quite simply, facilitators know people and relationships are vital. There is no substitute for the genuineness of a friend.

Charlotte Dingwall
Author, Facilitator, & Family Friend

All approaches require good facilitation. For example, in Karen's *one-to-one* family, the mother in their family and us as Karen's parents have been facilitators in the sense that we have made sure the friendships continue by supporting scheduling, providing encouragement, and monitoring the process. In the *social network* approach, a paid worker in Karen's life plays an important facilitation role, supporting Karen in her choices, and assisting her to expand her relationships. In Karen's *Circle*, parents and some friends play facilitating roles, such as being the organizer of meetings and monitoring follow-up actions. In the *bridging* approach, a facilitator assists Karen to connect with welcoming community settings based on her dreams. In *leisure identities*, the facilitator, who sometimes is a parent or friend, makes sure Karen has the equipment and resources needed to fulfill her interests and goals (i.e., drums, yoga mats, registration fees). More and more, for all five types of friendship building, Karen, with her strong desire for self-determination, is her own facilitator.

Sustainability

The final theme we have noticed that crossed all five approaches to friendship building is sustainability. Efforts toward building friends with Karen that have been strongest have been durable and continuing in nature. The *one-to-one* family friendship is now a 25 year relationship. Church, part of the *social network* approach, has been continuing for 20 years. The *Circle* is 20 years old with several original members still involved. Friends from work, formed from the *bridging* approach, are long standing. Karen's involvement in yoga, one of her *leisure identities*, is now in its 8th year and includes a wide variety of relationships.

> Good friends are like stars, you don't always
> see them, but you know they are there.
>
> Anonymous

The point is that having friends has been one of the most important dreams for Karen, her family, and friends. They have known it is an essential part of living an inclusive life. Ensuring that friendships happen takes a lot of commitment, focus, time, energy, educating, and resources. Strategies that are more longstanding in nature have higher pay-offs.

Conclusion: Beyond Labelling

Our friend Judith Snow has taught us that when we have a fully inclusive society, a focus on the person's disability disappears. However, we believe that many of Karen's friends over the years have had the experience of seeing Karen "as a person."

When this full acceptance happens, Karen's close friends simply see her as a person who loves to do art and yoga and swim and who happens to need support because she has a disability. It works because they acknowledge her difference and embrace ALL of her. They see her as a citizen making a contribution through being in the choir, community band, or working at the cafe. They see her as a person who is kind, gentle, a good listener, and enthusiastic. They see her as a person. And they see her as their friend.

Friends & Inclusion

Reference Notes
by Chapter

INTRODUCTION NOTES

[1] Pahl, R. (2000). On friendship. Cambridge: Polity Press.

Adams, R., Blieszner, R., & de Vries, B. (2000). Definitions of friendship in the third age: Age, gender, and study location effects. Journal of Aging Studies, 14(1), 117-133.

Bagwell, C., Newcomb, A., & Bukowski, W. (1998). Preadolescent friendship and peer rejection as predictors of adult adjustment. Child Development, 69(1), 140-153.

Cocking, D., & Kennett, J. (1998). Friendship and the self. Ethics, 109(3), 502-527.

Collins, A., Laursen, B., & Hartup, W. (Eds.). (1999). Relationships as developmental contexts. Philadelphia, PA: Laurence Erlbaum Associates/Taylor & Francis Group.

Feiring, C. (1999). Other-Sex friendship networks and the development of romantic relationships in adolescence. Journal of Youth and Adolescence, 28(4), 495-512.

Green, E. (1998). Women doing friendship': An analysis of women's leisure as a site of identity construction, empowerment and resistance, Leisure Studies, 17(3), 171-185.

Helsen, M., Vollebergh, W., & Meeus, W. (2000). Social support from parents and friends and emotional problems in adolescence. Journal of Youth and Adolescence, 29(3), 319-335.

Kingwell, M. (2001). The world we want: Virtue, vice and the good citizen. Toronto: Penguin Canada.

Leenders R. (1997). Evolution of friendship and best friend choice. In P. Doreien & F. Stokman (Eds.), Evolution of social networks (pp. 149-164). London: Routledge.

Sherman, A., de Vries, B., & Lansford, J. (1999). Friendship in childhood and adulthood: Lessons across the lifespan. The International Journal of Aging and Human Development, 51(1), 31-51.

Siebert, D., Mutran, E., & Reitzes, D. (1999). Friendship and social support: The importance of role identity to aging adults. Social Work, 44(6), 522-533.

Strauss, R., & Pollack, H. (2003). Social marginalization of overweight children. Archives of Pediatrics & Adolescent Medicine, 157(8), 746-752.

West, P., Sweeting, H., & Ecob, R. (1999). Family and friends' influences on the uptake of regular smoking from mid-adolescence to early childhood. Addiction, 94(9), 1397-1411.

[2] Amado, N. (Ed.). (1993). Friendships and community connections between people with and without developmental disabilities. Baltimore, MD: Paul Brookes Publishing.

Meyer, L., Park, H., Grenot-Scheyer, M., Schwartz, I., & Harry, B. (1998). Making friends: The influences of culture and development. Baltimore, MD: Paul Brookes Publishing Co.

Staub, D. (1998). Delicate threads: Friendships between children with and without special needs in inclusive settings. Bethesda, MD: Woodbine House Inc.

[3] Anniston, J. (2006). Community inclusion: People not just places. In K. Nankervis (ed.) Community disability services: An evidence based approach to practice .West Lafayette, IN: Purdue University Press.

Lord, J., & Hutchison, P. (2007). Pathways to inclusion: Building a new story with people and community. Toronto, ON: Captus Press.

McVilly, K., Stancliffe, R., Parmenter, T., & Burton-Smith, R. (2006). 'I get by with a little help from my friends:' Adults with intellectual disability discuss loneliness. Journal of Applied Research in Intellectual Disabilities, 19(2), 191-203.

[4] Wehmeyer, M. (1998). Self-determination and individuals with significant disabilities. Research and Practice for Persons with Severe Disabilities, 23(1), 5-16.

[5] Hutchison, P. (1990. Making friends: Developing relationships between people with a disability and other members of the community. Toronto: G. Allan Roeher Institute.

Hutchison, P. (2006). Leisure and disability. In R. McCarville, & J. MacIntosh (Eds.), Leisure for Canadians (pp.185-191). State College, PA: Venture Press.

Hutchison, P., & Lord, J. (1979). Recreation integration: Issues and alternatives in leisure services and community involvement. Toronto, ON: Leisurability Publications Inc. (also in French).

[6] Wilkinson, R., & Pickett, K. (2009). The spirit level: Why more equal societies almost always do better. Allen Lane Publisher.

[7] Taylor, A., Sylvestre, J., & Botschner, J. (1998). Social support is something you do, not something you provide: Implications for linking formal and informal support. Journal of Leisurability, 25(4), 3-13.

Rowlands, A. (2000). Understanding social support and friendship: Implications for intervention after acquired brain injury. Brain Impairment, 1(2), 151-164.

[8] Sciberras, J., & Hutchison, P. (2004). Friendships of youth with disabilities: Parents as partners. Leisure/Loisir, 28(1/2), 87-114.

[9] Chadsey, J., & Beyer, S. (2001). Social relationships in the workplace. Mental Retardation Developmental Disabilities Research Reviews, 7(2), 128-133.

[10] Hutchison, P., Mecke, T., & Sharpe, E. (2008). Partners in inclusion at a residential summer camp: A case study. Therapeutic Recreation, 42(3), 179-186.

[11] Pedlar, A., Haworth, L., Hutchison, P., Taylor, A. & Dunn, P. (1999). A

textured life: Empowerment and adults with developmental disabilities . Waterloo, ON: Laurier Press, p. 11.

[12] Reinders, J. (2002). The good life for citizens with intellectual disability. Journal of Intellectual Disability Research, 46(1), 1-5.

[13] Hutchison, P., & Lord, J. (1979). Recreation integration: Issues and alternatives in leisure services and community involvement. Toronto, ON: Leisurability Publications Inc. (also in French).

ONE-TO-ONE NOTES

[1] www.bigbrothersbigsisters.ca

[2] De Wit, D., Lipman, E., Manzano-Munguia, M., Bisanz, J., Graham, K., Offord, D., O'Neill, E., Pepler, D., & Shaver, K. (2006). Feasibility of a randomized controlled trial for evaluating the effectiveness of the Big Brothers Big Sisters community match program at the national level. Children and Youth Services Review, 29(3), 283-404.

Jekielek, S., Moore, K., Hair, E., & Scarupa, H. (2002, February). Mentoring: A promising strategy for youth development. Trends: Child Research Brief, www.mentoring.ca.gov/pdf/ MentoringBrief2002.pdf

[3] Peer tutors, Wikipedia, January 25, 2009

Gillespie, P., & Lerner, N. (2000). The Allyn and Bacon Guide to Peer Tutoring. Needham Heights, MA: Allyn and Bacon.

[4] Houston-Wilson, C., Dunn, J., van der Mars, H., & McCubbin, J. (1997). The effects of peer tutors on motor performance in integrated physical education classes. Adapted Physical Activity Quarterly, 14(4), 373-391.

[5] Centre for Learning and Literacy (1997, April 17). What is reading buddies? www.cll@unr.edu

[6] Carter, E., Cushing, L., Clark, N., & Kennedy, C. (2005). Effects of peer

support interventions on students' access to general curriculum and social interactions. Research and Practice for Persons with Severe Disabilities, 30(1), 15-25. In this article, it was shown that sometimes two peers relative to one peer was more beneficial peer support intervention.

Uditsky, B. (1993). From integration to inclusion: The Canadian experience. In R. Slee (Ed.). Is there a desk with my name on it: The politics of integration (pp. 79-92). New York: Routledge.

[7] Best Buddies International   www.bestbuddies.org

Options, R. Community living arrangements. www.academic.cengage.com

[8] Best Buddies Canada www.bestbuddies.ca

[9] Smith, C. (2002). Best Buddies: A comprehensive training programme introducing a peer buddy system to support students starting secondary school. UK: Sage Publications.

Harman, M., & Clark, C. (2006). Promoting friendship through Best Buddies: A national survey of college program participants. Mental Retardation, 44(1), 56-63.

Lehman, B. (2002). Evaluating the "Best Buddies" program: The influence of friendships on attitudes toward students. Claremont, CA: Claremont Graduate University.

West, M., Wehman, P. B., & Wehman, P. (2005). Competitive employment outcomes for persons with intellectual and developmental disabilities: The national impact of the Best Buddies Jobs Program. Journal of Vocational Rehabilitation, 23(1), 51-63.

[10] Gold, D. (1988). A look at Leisure Buddy programs. In D. Gold & J. McGill The pursuit of leisure. Toronto: G. Allan Roeher Institute.

[11] Extend a Family Waterloo Region www.eafwr.on.ca

[12] Hutchison, P., & McGill, J. (1998). Leisure, integration, and community (2nd ed.). Toronto, ON: Leisurability Publications (p. 303).

SOCIAL NETWORK NOTES

[1] Degenne, A., & Forse, M. (1999). Introducing social networks. Thousand Oaks, CA: Sage Publications.

[2] www.istheory.yorku.ca/socialnetworktheory.htm.

Scott, J. Social network analysis: A handbook (2nd ed.). Thousand Oaks, CA: Sage Publications.

www.en.Wikipedia.org/wiki/social_network

Belle, D. (1989). Children's social networks and supports. John Wiley.

[3] Wellman, B. (2001). The persistence and transformation of community: From neighbourhood groups to social networks. Report to the Law Commission of Canada. Toronto, ON: Wellman Associates.

[4] Lipsky, D., & Garter, A. (2004). Equity requires inclusion: The future for all students with disabilities. In D. Mitchell (ed.). Special educational needs and inclusive education (pp. 45-55). UK: Taylor & Francis.

[5] Fuchs, D., Fuchs, L. & Heward, (2000). Inclusion versus full inclusion. In W. Heward (ed.). Exceptional children: An introduction to special education. Upper Saddle River, NJ: Prentice Hall.

Stainback, W., & Stainback, S. (1990). Support networks for inclusive schooling: Interdependent integrated education. Baltimore, MD: Paul Brookes.

Guralnick, M. (1999). The nature and meaning of social integration for young children with mild developmental delays. Journal of Early Intervention, 22(1), 70-86.

[6] Forrester-Jones, R., Jones, S.., Heason, S., & DiTerizzi, M. (2004). Supported employment: A route to social networks. Journal of Applied Research in Intellectual Disabilities, 17(3), 199-208.

[7] Hutchison, P., & McGill, J. (1998). Leisure, integration, and community (2nd ed.). Toronto, ON: Leisurability Publications. p. 310.

[8] Wheatley, M., & Frieze, D. (2006). Lifecycle of emergence: Using emergence to take social innovation to scale, Berkana Institute, p. 1.

CIRCLES NOTES

[1] Oxfordshire Learning Disability Partnership Board. (n.d.). What is a Circle of support? www.Circlesnetwork.org.uk

[2] Lord, J., & Hutchison, P. (2007). Pathways to inclusion: Building a new story with people and community. Toronto, ON: Captus Press.

[3] Jansson, W., Almberg, B., Grafstrom, M., & Winblad, B. (1999). The Circle model: Support for relatives of people with dementia. International Journal of Geriatric Psychiatry, 13(10), 674-681.

Wilson, R., & Prinzo, M. (2001). Circles of support: A restorative justice initiative. Journal of Psychology and Human Sexuality, 13(3/4), 59-77.

[4] Perske, R., & Perske, M. (1988). Circle of friends: People with disabilities and their friends enrich the lives of one another. Burlington, ON: Welsh Publishing Co.

Mount, B., Beeman, P., & Ducharme, G. (1988). What are we learning about Circles of support? Connecticut: Communitas.

[5] Pearpoint, J. (1991). From behind the piano: The building of Judith Snow's unique Circle of friends. Toronto: Inclusion Press.

[6] Falvey, M., Forest, M., Pearpoint, J., & Rosenberg, R. (1997). All my life's a Circle: Using the tools: Circles, MAPS & PATHS. Toronto: Inclusion Press.

Jay, N. (2003). The Circles Network CREDO Project. Support for learning, 18(1), 24-28.

Joyce, S. (n.d.). Collage: Sketches of a support Circle. London, ON: Relations.

Newton, C., & Wilson, D. (2003). Creating Circles of friends: A peer support and inclusion workbook. Nottingham, UK: Inclusive Solutions.

[7] Gold, D. (1994). "We don't call it a 'Circle'": The ethos of a support group. Disability & Society, 9(4), 935-452(18).

Turnbull, A., Pereira, L., & Blue-Banning, M. (1999). Parents' facilitation of friendships between their children with a disability and friends without a disability. The Journal of the Association of Persons with Severe Disabilities, 24(2), 85-99.

Miller, M., Cooke, N., Test, D., & White, R. (2004). Effects of friendship Circles on the social interactions of elementary age students with mild disabilities. Journal of Behavioral Education, 12(3), 167-184.

Barrett, W. (2004). Investigating the Circle of friends approach: Adaptations and implications for practice. Educational Psychology in Practice, 20(4), 353-368.

Frederickson, N., Warren, L., & Turner, J. (2005). "Circle of Friends"- An exploration of impact over time. Educational Psychology in Practice, 21(3), 197-217.

Kalyva, E., & Avramidis, E., (2005). Improving communication between children with autism and their peers through the 'Circle of Friends': A small scale intervention study. Journal of Applied Research in Intellectual Disabilities, 18(3), 253-261.

Liu, F., Goodvin, S., Hummel, C., & Nance, E. (2008). An appreciative inquiry into the Circle of Friends Program: The benefits of social inclusion of students with disabilities. International Journal of Whole Schooling, 4(2), online.

[8] Falvey, M., Forest, M., Pearpoint, J., & Rosenberg, R. (1997). All my life's a Circle: Using the tools: Circles, MAPS & PATHS. Toronto: Inclusion Press. The eight steps are: 1. What is a MAP: 2. What is the person's history; 3. What are your dreams? 4. What are your nightmares? 5. Who is the person? 6. What are the person's strengths, gifts, or talents? 7. What does the person need? 8. What is the plan of action?

[9] Ibid.

BRIDGING NOTES

[1] Oldenburg, R. (1999). Cafes, coffee shops, bookstores, bars, hair salons, and other hangouts at the heart of a community. Cambridge, MA: Da Capo Press.

[2] McKnight, J. (1992). Beyond community services: The careless society. New York: Basic Books.

Walker, P. (1999). From community presence to sense of place: Community experiences of adults with developmental disabilities. Journal of the Association for Persons with Severe Handicaps, 24(1), 23-32.

[3] Putman, R. (2000). Bowling alone: The collapse and revival of American community. New York: Simon & Schuster.

Putnam, R., & Feldstein, M. (2003). Better together: Restoring the American community. New York: Simon & Schuster.

[4] Schwartz, D. (1997). Who cares? Re-discovering community. Boulder, CO: Westview Press.

Friedland, L., & Morimoto, S. (2006). The lifeworlds of young people and civic engagement. In P. Levine & J. Youniss (ed.). Youth civic engagement: An institutional turn (pp. 37-39). Medford, MA: The Centre for Information & Research on Civic Learning & Engagement.

Longo, N. (2007). Why community matters: Connecting education and civic life. Albany, NY: SUNY Press.

[5] Laurier, E., Philo, C. (2005). The Cappuccino community: Cafes and civic life in the contemporary city. Glasgow, Scotland: Dept. Of Geography & Topographic Science, University of Glasgow.Cattell, V., Dines, N., Gesler, W., & Curtis, S. (2007). Mingling, observing, and lingering: Everyday public spaces and their implications for well-being and social relations. Healthplace, 14(3), 544-561.

Frazee, R. (2001). The connecting church: Beyond small groups to authentic community. Grand Rapids, MI: Zondervan Publisher.

Leydon, K. (2003). Social capital and the built environment: The importance of walkable neighbourhoods, American Journal of Public Health, 93(9), 1546-1551.

[6] Ludlum, C. (2002). One candle power: Seven principles that enhance lives of people with disabilities and their communities. Toronto: Inclusion Press.

Hutchison, P., & McGill, J. (1998). Leisure, integration, and community (2nd ed.). Toronto, ON: Leisurability Publications.

Kretzmann, J., McKnight, J., & Turner, N. (1996). Voluntary associations in low-income neighbourhoods: An unexplored community resource. Evanston, IL: Institute for Policy Research, Northwestern University.

[7] Amado, A., Conklin, F., & Wells, J. (1990). Friends: A manual for connecting persons with disabilities and community members. St. Paul, MN: Human Services Research and Development Centre.

[8] City of Seattle Department of Neighborhoods. (2000). Involving all neighbours: Building inclusive communities in Seattle. Seattle: Author.

[9] Johannes, A., & Kurliak, S. (2009). 101 ways to make friends: Ideas and conversation starters for people with disabilities and their supporters. Vancouver, BC: Spectrum Society for Community Living.

[10] Kretzmann, J., & McKnight, J. (1993). Building communities from the inside out: A path toward finding and mobilizing a community's assets. Evanston, IL: Asset-Based Community Development Institute, p. 6

Kretzmann, J., McKnight, J., Sheehan, G., & Green, M. (1997). A guide to capacity inventories: Mobilizing the community skills of local residents. Evanston, IL: Asset-Based Community Development Institute.

Kretzmann, J., McKnight, J., & Puntenney, D. (2005). Discovering community power: A guide to mobilizing local assets and your organization's capacity. Chicago: Asset-Based Community Development Institute.

Turner, N., Kretzmann, J., & McKnight, J. (1999). A guide to mapping and mobilizing the associations in local neighbourhoods. Chicago: Asset-Based Community Development Institute.

LEISURE IDENTITIES NOTES

[1] Eccles, J. (2005). Activity choices in middle childhood: The roles of gender, self-belief, and parents' influence. In J. Mahoney, R. Larsen,

J. Eccles (Eds.). Organized activities as contexts of development: Extracurricular activities, afterschool and community programs (pp. 235-).London: Routledge.

[2] Stebbins, R. (2006). Serious leisure: A perspective for our time. Piscataway: NJ: Transaction Publishers.

Stebbins, R. (2004). Between work and leisure: The common ground of two separate worlds. Piscataway: NJ: Transaction Publishers.

Stebbins, R. (1992). Amateurs, professionals, and serious leisure. Montreal and Kingston: McGill-Queen's University Press.

Stebbins, R. (1977). The amateur: Two sociological definitions. Pacific Sociological Review, 20(4), 582-606.

[3] Gillespie, D., Leffler, A., & Lerner, E. (2002). If it weren't my hobby, I'd have a life: Dog sports, serious leisure, and boundary negotiations. Leisure Studies, 21(3/4), 285-384.

Jones, I., & Green, C. (2006). Serious leisure, social identity and sport tourism. In H. Gibson (ed.). Sport tourism: Concepts and theories (pp. 32-49). London: Routledge

[4] Caldwell, L., & Baldwin, C. (2003). A serious look at leisure: The role of leisure time and recreation activities in positive youth. In F. Villarruel, D. Perkins, L. Borden, & J. Keith (eds.). Community youth development: Programs, policies and practices (pp. 181-200). Thousand Oaks, CA: Sage.

Brown, C., McGuire, F., & Voelkl, J. (2008). The link between successful aging and serious leisure. The International Journal of Aging and Human Development, 66(1), 73-95.

[5] Stebbins, R. (2001). Serious leisure. Society, 38(4), 53-57.

[6] Stebbins, R. (2008). Right leisure: Serious, casual, or project-based. Neuro-rehabilitation, 23(4), 335-341.

[7] McGill, J. (1996). Developing leisure identities: A pilot project. Brampton, ON: Brampton Caledon Community Living.

CONCLUSION: NOTES

[1] Arntz, W., Chasse, B., & Vincente, M. (2005). What the bleep do we know!? Discovering the endless possibilities for altering your everyday reality. Deerfield Beach, FL: Health Communications Inc.

[2] Whitaker, P., Barratt, P., Joy, H., Potter, M., & Thomas, G. (2003). Children with autism and peer group support: Using circles of friends. British Journal of Special Education, 25(2), 60-64.

[3] Turnbull, A., & Turnbull, R. (2006). Self-determination: Is a rose by any other name still a rose? Research and Practice for Persons with Severe disabilities, 31(1), 1-6.

Hickson, M. (2008). The meanings of close friendship: The views of four people with intellectual disabilities. Journal of Applied Research in Intellectual Disabilities, 14(3), 276-291.

[4] Williams, M. (2001). The 10 lenses: Your guide to living & working in a multicultural world. Stirling, VA: Capitol Books.

Sieber, E. (2003). Women in literature: Reading through the lens of gender. Westport, CN: Greenwood Publishing.

[5] McKnight, J. (1992). Beyond community services: The careless society. New York: Basic Books.

Walker, P. (1999). From community presence to sense of place: Community experiences of adults with developmental disabilities. Journal of the Association for Persons with Severe Handicaps, 24(1), 23-32.

[6] Buysse, V., Goldman, B., & Skinner, M. (2002). Setting effects on friendship formation among young children with and without disabilities, Exceptional Children, 64(4), 503-517.

Knox, M., & Hickson, F. (2001). The meanings of close friendship: The views of four people with intellectual disabilities. Journal of Applied Research in Intellectual Disabilities, 14(3), 276-291.

[7] Lord, J., & Hutchison, P. (2007). Pathways to inclusion: Building a new story with people and community. Toronto, ON: Captus Press.

Burgin, D. (2003). Facilitators and barriers to incorporating students with disabilities into the general education. Johnson City, TN: East Tennessee State University.

Pickering, S. (2001). Working with communities. In J. Thompson & S. Pickering (Eds.). Meeting the health needs of people who have a learning disability (pp. 306-319). Philadelphia, PA: Elsevier Health Sciences Publishing.

[8] Turnbull, A., Pereira, L., & Blue-Banning, M. (2000). Teachers as friendship facilitators. Teaching Exceptional Children, 32(5), 66-70.

Cook, J. (2001). Facilitating friendships for children with disabilities. Focal Point, 15(2), 9-10.

Schaffner, C., & Buswell, B. (1992). Connecting students: A guide to thoughtful friendship facilitation for educators & families. PEAK Parent Centre

Peggy Hutchison and John Lord are parents of Karen Lord.

Peggy is a retired professor who has taught, researched and advocated for inclusion and friendship for many years.

John is an inclusion researcher and facilitator and a partner in the Facilitation Leadership Group.

Karen is active in her community as a self-advocate, yoga teacher, employee of several work places, and lectures about inclusion and friendship.

John and Peggy were co-founders of the Centre for Community Based research and have authored numerous publications. All three live in Kitchener-Waterloo.

Authors can be contacted through John's website **www.johnlord.net**

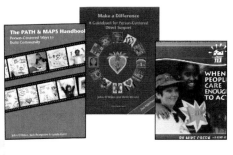

- **PATH & MAPS Handbook:** Person-Centered Ways to Build Community (NEW)
- **Gentle Heart Fearless Mind:** Mindfulness DVD + Booklet: Alan Sloan (NEW)
- **Friends & Inclusion:** Five Approaches to Building Relationships: P. Hutchison; J. Lord, K. Lord (NEW)
- **Make a Difference Pack:** Leader's Manual + MAD Guidebook +10 Learning Journey Booklets
- **Golden Reflections:** - written by Vargus Yale (Mike's seeing-eye guide dog) with Mike Yale
  Also available in Audio MP3 read by Don Herron and as a package with the book
- **Inclusive Education: Emergent Solutions** Gary Bunch & Angela Valeo
- **Planning for a Real Life After School: Transition from School (2 editions)**
- **The Poetry of David Moreau:** If You're Happy and You Know It Clap Your Hand
- **Doing Our Best Work:** 10 Ingredients of Quality Support: Peter Leidy - DVD
- **ABCD in Action - DVD & Book -When People Care Enough to Act**
- **My Life My Choice - DVD - Seven Adults living full lives in the community**
- **Make a Difference - book; Leaders Guide, Work Booklets**
- **The Big Plan - A Good Life After School - Transition Planning with groups**
- **Each Belongs - book & CD - The 1st Inclusive School Board ever!**
- **PlayFair Teams - 2 books, DVD + Posters - blended teams in schools.**
- **Find Meaning in the Work - CD & Manual/Curriculum - presentation ready!**
- **Free to Fly - A Story of Manic Depression - Caroline Fei-Yeng Kwok**
- **Supporting Learners with Intellectual Challenge -teacher resources**

INCLUSION PRESS

47 Indian Trail, Toronto,

Ontario Canada M6R 1Z8

p. 416.658.5363 f. 416.658.5067

e. inclusionpress@inclusion.com

inclusion.com BOOKS • WORKSHOPS • MEDIA • RESOURCES